THE DETERMINED DAYS

THE DETERMINED DAYS

PHILIP STEPHENS

SEWANEE WRITERS' SERIES / THE OVERLOOK PRESS

First published in the United States in 2000 by
The Overlook Press, Peter Mayer Publishers, Inc.
Lewis Hollow Road
Woodstock, NY 12498
www.overlookpress.com

Grateful acknowledgment is made to the following journals in which these
poems first appeared:

Agni: "True Story"
Alabama Literary Review: "Blue Rose Motel," "Paradise, Missouri," "Stripper"
The Journal: "The Signalmen"
Meridian: "Commute," "The Ordered Life"
The North American Review: "God Shed His Grace"
Sewanee Theological Review: "Hangman"
Southwest Review: "Vineyard"

"Ditch Digging," "Climbing," and Section III first appeared as the 1999 win-
ner of the St. Louis Poetry Center's Hanks Chapbook Award under the title
The Signalmen.

Library of Congress Cataloging-in-Publication Data

Stephens, Philip.
The determined days : poems / Philip Stephens.
p. cm.
I. Title.
PS3569.T4518D48   2000   811'.6—dc21   00-025743

Book design and type formatting by Bernard Schleifer
Manufactured in the United States of America
First Edition
1 3 5 7 9 8 6 4 2
ISBN 1-58567-014-6

ACKNOWLEDGMENTS

I wish to offer my thanks to Rachel Hadas, Anthony Hecht, Amy Hempel, John Hollander, Andrew Hudgins, Mark Jarman, Donald Justice, Charles Martin, Erin McGraw, Cheri Peters, Wyatt Prunty, and Sherod Santos for their encouragement and guidance during the writing of these poems. Thanks also to Bob Jones for his meticulous eye.

For their long-standing friendship, advice, and patience I owe my limitless yet insufficient gratitude to Daniel Anderson, Jennie Hanna, and Greg Williamson.

For my parents, Carl and Judy Stephens

C O N T E N T S

Seeing his days *are* determined,
the number of his months *are* with thee,
thou hast appointed his bounds that he cannot pass:
Turn from him, that he may rest,
till he shall accomplish, as an hireling, his day.

Job 14:5-6

DITCH DIGGING

We—Hondo, Hawk, Smith, Sandoval, and Rome—
Stab with our picks and shovels at the loam,
The sand, black stones the size of hearts, then clay.
Layer by stubborn layer, we make our way
Half of a grave's depth down into the earth.
We sculpt a narrow ditch, for what it's worth,
And then we lay pipe, glue it, backfill in.
Next day, where that pipe stops, we start again.
And so on: pick and shovel, shovel, pick.
Steel blades thrust at the sticky grit go *tick*,
Chunk, tick, chunk, tick, the dreary, grating sound
Of rusted clock gears winding, finally, down.
If we were to look up we might observe
The main line, raw and quivering like a nerve,
The ganglia of spurs, the gleam of flies
Over a dead rat, piles of rotten ties,
Illegals by a boxcar boiling clothes,
Laborers stooping through the garlic rows,
And intermittent freight trains hurtling by
The cruciform poles stuck against the sky.
So we keep to the dirt and stony stacks
And kill the time by bitching about our backs,
The weather, foremen, union dues, or the jerk
Who drives by each day yelling *work, work*.
Spare me those fanfares for the common grunts.
Ditch digging's just the shit work no one wants.
It isn't science, and it isn't art.

Quite senselessly, we pick some earth apart
And put it back, almost like before.
Nothing changes. Nothing. Nothing more
Except when day ends, Rome might tell a joke,
And we'll drink coffee, chew, or have a smoke,
Turning our backs on the little sinking scar
Of broken dirt that leads to where we are.

I

HANGMAN

Snow falls so hard the neighbors' windows seem
To stare at me through viscid cataracts,
And so I feel like I'm watched but unseen.
She's gone. The strokes took her away piecemeal:
Her reasoning failed, her left side lost all feeling,
But on the good days she'd ask where I was.
"Right here," I'd say. That answer didn't suit her,
So I'd ask her where I was: "Hunting quail,"
She'd say, or "playing poker," things I did
Before we married. Sometimes she'd mistake me
For suitors I'd contended with in school,
Or she'd hallucinate events from childhood:
A grassfire down the street, the shell-shocked soldier
Who swept the floor each night in Dunstan's Drugs,
Leeches she scraped barehanded from her shins
After she'd skinny-dipped in Francis Branch.
So quickly she regressed I thought of dolls
One twists apart to find another doll,
Another, and another, until what's left
Is nothing, the last piece lost some years ago.
Each day, though, I remain at my routine:
The morning paper's crossword, cups of coffee,
Then errands, supper, reading, and to bed.
But with this snow, the streets have disappeared.
It seems too soon for snow. I set out bowls
Of candy last night, like she always did,
But was disturbed when children rang the bell.

Swaddled in sheets, baring plastic fangs,
Laden with besoms, they cried *trick or treat*
As if the night were some uproarious joke.
It started snowing harder, and they vanished.
My neighbors turned their porch lights out, but still,
Teenagers from the run-down neighborhood
Just blocks from here kept knocking at the doors.
They wore jeans, hooded sweatshirts, and they stared
Through me unless I asked, "Where are your costumes?"
One of them always said: "These are our costumes."
This morning, thumbing to the crossword puzzle,
I read that in that neighborhood, a man
Fashioned a noose from an extension cord
Then climbed up in a tree in his front yard
And hanged himself. The corpse remained for days.
The neighbors thought it was a decoration,
Bound straw or newsprint dressed to scare the kids.
Without her, I've not finished many crosswords.
She'd putter in the kitchen while I called
For answers to the clues I couldn't get:
Eight letters, for example, river islands;
Or seven letters, pardon; or nine letters,
Ends with an *n*, a system of ID.
And thus, in turn, we'd fill the empty spaces,
Which is what pleased me, grids laid down like maps,
Lone letters as mysterious as runes,
Until each word or phrase we had to link
With ordinary human life was formed:
Sandbars or *amnesty* or *Bertillon*.
But I've been thinking of that children's game
Which takes two players. One knows the solution,

Draws lines for every letter of the phrase,
And then a bare-boned scaffold and a rope.
The other chooses letters that might fill
The blanks; however, with the first wrong choice
A circle's drawn below the rope, the next
Wrong choice, a line, and then more lines until
A human figure hangs, just as some nights
Like this, while snow erases all the streets,
A spindling dark form dangles from a branch—
A lower case *l* scratched inside a square,
Hinting at words like *life* or *loan* or *loss*.
No. It's an effigy in casual clothes
And at each gust, it kicks. What's it made of?
Old straw bound up with twine, the *Times*, the wind?

MARCH

Behind a rack piled high with pastel tax forms,
Two men shed gloves, soiled coats, and the frayed mail
Of cardigans they'd scrounged for, then sat down.
One leaned across the table, whispered, "Virge,
Are you sure they can't see us?"

                              "Dundee, I swear,
I'm telling you those papers make a wall."

But Dundee glanced around. The unemployed
Flipped through the classifieds; retirees shuffled
Past shelves of history. Dundee shrugged.
He reached beneath his sweatshirt and withdrew
A box, shook off the top, laid down a board
Where each man lined his rank and file, then moved:
Pawns out, then knights or bishops, one pawn swept
Aside like it was never there, then, "Virge,
You know how you said you'd like just one chance?"

"Uh huh."

                   "Well, I know how. Near Union Mission
At this house called Men's Place, you get a room,
Three squares, a job. They even let you stay
Long as you like, but it don't cost you nothing.
Just all you got to do is get the word
Of God."

                "What do you mean I got to get it?"

"You know. You got to beg for God's forgiveness."

"What's God got to forgive me for? He needs
To beg for my forgiveness, is what he needs
To beg." Their pieces clattered: knight takes rook
And queen takes knight, each loss turned into gain.

"A guy I know that lives there's got a board,
But he don't know the rules."

                          "You think you do?
I've got your queen. You want to quit?"

                                "I don't.
We could get jobs. It ain't so much to get
The word of God."

                    "It's just the same if you
Got God's good word or not. Some winter nights
I've sat my black ass on a pew and prayed
With other souls until they let us eat,
But if they got no room then we get put
Outside, where, if God's there, he's one cold bitch.
But if they got room, we can't drink or smoke,
Can't make a sound. You've seen the crazy fools,
Yelling like they was wounded, get pitched out.
So much for God's good word. It ain't no chance.
And looky there. Man, you ain't got one now.
Rook's got you—bishop too."

                          "Virge. Virge."

A woman spoke: "If you men want to stay,
Take up a book and please be quiet."

                                "Quiet?"
Virge said. "Quiet? I ain't disturbed a soul."

BLUE ROSE MOTEL

They ducked out of the rain blown off the gutter.
The door clicked shut. "Shh. Listen," Helen said.

"To what?" Ward said, but Helen scanned the room.

"Let's just go on."

                    "You said stop. So I stopped.
Did you want something swank between Des Moines
And Kansas City?" Helen bit her lip.
"Oh, c'mon. What's the matter now? I mean,
All I said was I wished you hadn't told me
This thing you told me before we made the trip.
Then you got mad."

                    "Why shouldn't I? You're scared
Of what your folks'll think."

                              "No. All I said
Was that I thought it would be easier
To take this visit, not knowing what I know."

"Why can't you say it, Ward?"

                         "Look. I can say it,
But this is not the time to have it out.
My parents find out how you are, they'll think—"

"I know what they'll think. They'll think some white trash
Has got her money-grubbing claws in you.
I don't care what they think. I care what you think."

Ward turned, and curtains strung across the doorway
Behind the counter bellied up and split,
Unveiling a thick-gutted man who stuck
His uppers out, then sucked them back and scowled:
"You need a room? Or you just want directions?"

"A room," Ward said.

                "Reason I ask you that
Is ain't nobody stops." The old man passed
A pen and form to Ward, then took his card.
From back where Helen waited, she could glimpse,
Between the gaping curtains, TV light—
First peach, then pink, red, brown, the close-up shot,
Or so it seemed, of some exotic flower.
"My wife, she said the sky was heavy here.
That's why nobody'd stop. She wasn't right
Up in her head, though. Lord, a night like this
Would make her crazy as a shithouse rat."

"What's that?" said Helen.

                    Ward looked up. "What's what?"
"That screaming."

              "I don't hear a thing."

                      "I do."

"This old boy keeps a mare across the four-lane.
She's foaling."

            "Does he know that?" Helen said.
The old man stared. "I mean, what if she's narrow?
What if her colt's breech?"

"You some farm-fed girl?"
The old man said. Ward didn't speak to that;
He kept his head down, filling out the forms
While Helen focused on the TV screen,
Glimpsing robed women kneeling on a stage.
They gripped another woman who was naked
And struggling as a black man mounted her.
Ward passed the form back, and the old man's teeth
Clicked as he said, "My wife begged me to call
This place the Green Rose, but there's no such thing.
'Somewhere there is,' she'd say. We come to find
There ain't no blue ones neither. Here's your key."

"I'll get the car," Ward said, then he was gone.

"I built us this blue rose," the old man said,
"Some thirty-foot high out of fiberglass
To draw the tourists in. Wind blew it down."
The old man stuck his lower plate toward Helen.
She looked away from him and saw the screen,
The woman balanced on a low trapeze
While men in crotchless tights were hoisted toward her.
Ward honked, and Helen turned, but out beyond
The four-lane, headlights cut across the field.
"Looks like they got that mare," the old man said.

VINEYARD

"Six feet, huh?" Bodie Heller asked.

                                  "That's right,"
My uncle said while we walked past bare vines
That clung to trellis wires like worn-out men.

"You measure if you want," the old man said.
"I know six feet." He swung his pick three times
Then paced the distance off and swung again.
We followed, digging clay, chucking stones,
And dropping spindly vines into the holes.

"You hear that whippoorwill up on your roof?"
I asked my uncle.

                    "Keep you awake?" he said.
"They will do that. They keep the bugs down, though."

"Up on your house?" said Bodie. "That's bad luck.
They say that whippoorwills are merciless souls
Crying for heaven. They say that souls get lost
And got to find things here to do."

                             "Bode drinks,"
My uncle whispered. "He's a worker, though."

"Six feet is how deep we dug graves at Dooley,"
Said Bodie. "That's hard work. It's rock and clay
And cold clear down."

                   "This ground's not any good
For grapes or graves, huh Bode?" my uncle said.

"I dug my baby's grave," was Bodie's answer.
"You dig a baby's like a man's. Six feet.
My wife, she used to say I'd brought the dead
Back from the graveyard. Said they took the baby."

"You don't believe that stuff," my uncle said.
"Do you?"

       "Don't know. I know I didn't make
Enough to feed a baby. I know that line
Between the dead and living's awful thin.
You know the only way they know a man
Is dead is hold a mirror to his nose?"

"The only way?" my uncle said. "Come on."

A cardinal flitted through the tangled walls
Of cedar, oak, and ghosts of blooming dogwood.
What cheer, cheer, cheer, he cried. A bobwhite called.
"You hear?" the old man said. "He knows. *Bode's right,*
He says. *Bode's right.*" Bodie worked up his row
Until he stopped across from us and said,
"Years back, me and this old boy dug a plot
For some piss-poor dirt farmer name of Shipley.
This banker, name of Wills, comes down next day,
Says Shipley's in the wrong plot—Wills's plot.
We dig that coffin up, and when we do,
We see the seal's broke. Course, we have a look.
And there's old Shipley, eyes as wide as dollars,
Blue flesh, a twisted face. Got his hands
Up here, and every fingertip's scraped off.
Well, all Wills says is, 'Looks like that old boy
Figured out he was in the wrong place too.'"

Bodie walked up the hill to get a shovel.
When he came back, he knelt and grabbed a vine.
"Looks dead," he said.

                              "It's not," my uncle said.
"It's green as grass."

                              "Just said it looks that way."
Then Bodie fished his pocketknife out, scored
The bark, and said, "Yessir." He dropped the vine
Into its hole then scraped and tamped the earth
With his bare hand. "Bode's right," he said. "Bode's right."

PUBLIC RELATIONS

A social worker asked if I'd produce
A video about this home for kids
Who've been abused. She told me it would play
For benefactors at a black-tie ball,
And that I'd have to keep it light or else
No one would donate money. I agreed.
At first we shot some b-roll on the grounds:
Clipped hedges, shafts of light through palmate leaves
Speckling the eggshell clapboards, sprinkler valves
Spitting chipped opals on begonia blooms.
Then, inside: coats hung on their pegs, small chairs
In semicircles, and crayon renderings
Of sky-blue houses. I chose not to shoot
Some other drawings: lizards wielding knives,
A house in crimson flames, and stickmen caught
And kicking through a lake thick with black spiders.
We filmed kids talking about what they wanted
To be when they grew up, and I enjoyed that,
But I was taken with this brown-haired girl
Who seemed both cool and forthright when I asked
If she'd tell me about her tempera painting
Of black trees in blue yards. "It's night," she said,
"Before it's night, when everyone's TVs
Get loud, and no one sees things very clear."
But then what struck me was the way she asked
Questions and listened so attentively
I caught myself explaining how I like

Photography much more than I like film.
"A photograph stops time," I said. "With film,
You have to live inside the medium."
When I packed up, I told the social worker
That girl would make the perfect daughter. "Yes,"
She said. "She's learned how men want her to be."
I didn't want to know more, but she told me
How that girl's father died in a freak car crash,
And some time after that her mother married
A high-school coach. The mother was a nurse.
On nights she worked, he took the school's AV
Equipment home and shot the girl pretending
She was a TV journalist, or actress.
Later, he coaxed her into sexual acts
And sold the videos out on the market.
"What you saw isn't her," the woman said.
"She's what he made. We can't get to her."
Godard once said the eye should learn to listen
Before it looks, and I believe that's true.
But image, people say, is everything,
And I think that's true too, for everything
At once is nothing I can comprehend.

THE HEADLESS DEER

If you can say you've never seen a ghost,
You wouldn't know if one walked up and bit you.
You're better off. I've lived alone for years,
And sometimes my own voice can make me jump
So high I have to get out of the house
And call on folks. But no one's here to see.
Only place left to go these days is Wal-Mart.
I've got old friends work there. We can't talk.
Mostly what I get out of them is, "Hi.
Welcome to Wal-Mart. May I help you?" Good God.
Don't they think I know where things are? I know.
That's what they're paid to say. I understand.
We used to work together, stitching pants
For soldiers in the war. At four o'clock,
I'd rise and fry a chicken for my husband
He'd take on runs he made for the Rock Island.
I'd fix him eggs and mush. I'd fill his thermos.
He'd leave, then I'd get dressed beside the stove
And go up to the factory by myself.
Come afternoon, we women walked together.
Our faces were so stained with sweat and lint
That we looked bruised; some were afraid of folks
Knowing they worked, and wouldn't cut down Main.
I would. I wasn't scared of anything.
But then some mornings just the stink of grease
And coffee'd make me sick. And so I knew.

My husband said, and I agreed, we'd need
More money with a baby on the way,
So I stayed on at work. I never told.
The women showed me how to hide my belly.
They took my slack, or else I'd have been fired.
I had a boy, just like my husband wanted,
Like most men want to carry on their names.
He died in childbirth. All my husband did
Was stand beside the bed and stare, real quiet,
Like I had died. I stayed in bed for weeks,
Until one dusk I got up, walked downstairs
Out to my garden and started picking beans.
Foxtail had clogged the rows, squash had rotted,
Tomatoes too. I knew the beans were hollow,
But I kept picking. Pines out back of here
That kept the train noise out when trains still ran
Started to rustle. A jay or squirrel, I thought,
But when I looked just down the row, I saw,
No further than a body's length from me,
A deer. It didn't have a head. It didn't.
A shattered bone, a half-healed scar. It twitched
Like flies were biting it and stood splay-legged
So long it seemed to watch me like folks do
When they can't place your name but know your face.
I reached for it, but it ran through the pines.
I shook so bad beans spilled out of my gown.
You want to know how that deer lost its head.
Folks used to say that in the Civil War
It got hit by a cannonball; they'd say
After the railroad came and folks moved here

From other towns for work, a freight train struck it.
Some say it's downtown, where the stores have closed.
It doesn't matter how it lost its head.
What matters is I saw it, and I've said so.

VISITOR

Racket the dogs made woke me after midnight.
That late, they're running deer out of the vines,
But it was pouring rain, and when there's weather,
They ain't inclined to move, so I got up.
I see this girl, or woman, really, huddled
Under the dripping eave beside the door.
I say, "Let me get decent," and I do,
Then sit her by the stove. But when she says,
"I'm sorry to have bothered you so late,"
Like we were old acquaintances or something,
I hear the dogs still barking at the road.
She's got that hippie look: long brownish hair,
Flowing peony-printed dress, workboots,
And this jean jacket she shucks off so fast
That when she asks if I'll drive her to town,
I'm standing stupid, staring at peonies.
"I got into it with some friends," she says.
"They kicked me out."

        "Where at?" I say.

                "Mile back

Or so," she says, but I can see her hair
Ain't even wet, and when she smoothes her dress
And sits up straight, I have to look away.
I shove the window up and call the dogs,
But when I do, it's then I catch her stealing
Glances around the room like she's lost something.

"You live 'round here?" I say. She folds her hands
Tight in her lap and says she's visiting
Her aunt in town.

            Before I ask, she says,
"You wouldn't know her, though. Keeps to herself."

"How 'bout we call her?" I say. "Have her get you?"
She says her aunt's sick. Cancer. She needs rest.
Outside, the grape leaves rattle in the rain,
Then one dog howls. "What you think's out there?" I say.
She shrugs and stands and sidles past real close,
So I say, "I don't like to leave here long."

"Shouldn't take long," she says.

                  I slip between
Her and the door, next to the phone, and tell her,
"'While back, somebody got in, took my guns.
Some folks think I've got things I don't, but look—
A black-and-white TV, that chair, wood stove."
But all she says is don't my wines make money.
I tell her how, years back, docs cracked my chest,
Winched back my ribs, and fiddled with my ticker;
They grafted, spliced, then told me take life easy.
But I went out, bought land, and planted vines
In dirt so poor you got to shovel horseshit
Around the phone poles just to get a dial tone.
What money I had left, my ex-wife got.
"She hated sweat," I say.

             So this girl says,
"There's lots of folks would like to have your life."

I say folks got this notion about vineyards

That grapes just hop in bottles and make wine.
But no, it's digging, planting, spraying, pruning—
Two runners for each vine, five spurs a runner,
Three buds a spur. You're lucky if your vines make.
Then if black rot don't get them, songbirds will.
I go on like that for awhile. She nods
And smiles until I say, "How 'bout I call
The sheriff? He's a friend of mine. He owes me."

"No, don't do that," she says.

                               I say, "Why not?"

She says she's on probation, but she's been
Falsely accused. "Friends with me did it," she says.
"Don't call, please. They'll just haul me off, and then
My aunt'll be alone."

                        "Who's with you now?"
I say, and she shuts up, and I can't stop
Staring at those peonies, thinking how
Those flowers look fleshy, pale, but get up close,
You see ants swarm each bloom like it's a dead thing.
I reach for the receiver.

                        Then she yells,
"You S.O.B.," and gets all goggle-eyed
And snatches up her jacket, scoots outside
Without a fare-thee-well, and disappears
Down through my vines. I call the dogs, lock up,
Turn out the lights, and then I watch my windows
Until my eyes can see the dark. She's out there.
Day I don't think she's coming, she'll be back.

THE ORDERED LIFE

With five men in grim suits much like my own,
Another in a chauffeur's hat, another
Sporting a wrinkled boutonniere, I stood
Outside and watched snow fall on trees so packed
With yellow leaves their limbs began to sag
And crack like rifles fired in celebration.
The hearse before us thrummed; its back hatch gaped.
The boutonniere fed flowers into it,
But when a limb two hundred feet away
Dropped on a line, he looked up, brushed his hands,
And spoke: "No power tonight."

                                        "There better be,"
The fat man by me said. "My freezer's full
Of eight-point buck. That's my good chili meat."
The men just nodded; the fat man turned to me.
"You got a permit?"

                        "Permit?" I said.

                                        "Deer.
We got so many, county threw this hunt
Down at the park last week. They flushed. We shot.
Kids 'bout your age come down here from the college.
Protesters. I can't see why they can't see
The reason there's so many deer is 'cause
We got too many folks down at the lake.
Too many folks runs off the predators.
Somebody's got to be a predator.
Except for Les there. Les couldn't hit a deer

If it was hung up in his closet."

"Shit,"
The boutonniere said. "Shit."

The fat man chuckled
And glanced back at the doors. "You related?"

"Nephew," I said.

"I didn't know her well.
My wife and her, they'd swap pain pills sometimes.
I never even been inside her house,
But they say every room still looks like new.
I hear she wouldn't let folks past the kitchen,
And even there, you had to take your shoes off."

"That right?" I said, though just that day I'd seen
Her pristine dresses hung by length and color,
Her shoes in rows, her draperies pressed, the fringe
Of Oriental rugs combed straight, lamps centered
On every table, and empty, dustless shelves.

"Look at my hands," the fat man said. "I swear,
When I wear suits I swell up like a drowned man."
He held his hands toward me, but then the doors
Behind us creaked—another boutonniere
Guided the coffin like a grocery cart,
So we grabbed hold and worked it in the hatch
Then climbed into a van that tailed the hearse
And limousine down sidestreets to the highway.
We passed my dead aunt's house: the brick front neat,
The lawn gone smooth, the oaks, though, rended, stripped.
"It's got to be this suit," the fat man said.
"Or catfish. Caught a mess on trotlines last night.

Took half my morning cleaning them. Their whiskers,
They say, are poison. You staying here tonight?"

"I have to catch a plane."

                              "You'll miss the fish fry.
Month back, this bigwig—carried lots of cash
And showed it off too much—just disappeared.
We're raising funds so they can keep on searching,
A favor for his wife. But they won't find him,
Not all of him."

                    The cemetery gates
Passed by, and while our meager cortege closed rank,
Les whispered, "Looky there." He pointed past
The white-capped stones, the tent that sheltered rows
Of folding chairs, the mourners wavering
Through grainy snow, and past the men who waited
Beside the backhoe, where three gaunt does stood
And watched us all. "I had my rifle," Les said,
"That'd be a sweet shot."

                              "Yeah," the fat man said.
"They couldn't pick a better place to be."

O w l   i n   t h e   S n o w

"What were you doing?" she said then followed him
To where he set his boots beside the heater.

"Checking the mail."

                    "I know that much. You said so.
I meant in the front field. That snow's knee deep.
You're not so young, you know. Something could happen."

"Good grief. I tracked some prints out in the snow."

"I meant when you fell back and rolled around.
I thought you'd had a heart attack."

                                        "Oh, that.
I made an angel in the snow, the way
The boys used to."

            She turned away from him
And took clipped steps back to her kitchen cabinets,
Which were flung out like wings. "You're bored, aren't you?
You've gone to check the mail four times today."

"Have I got you upset?"

                    "I'm not upset.
These mice. They eat their way through everything.
They've gone and tripped those traps you set last night."

He watched her snatch a few cans from the shelf
Then sat beside the window. "Getting dark.
I'll bet it snows some more."

                              "You never noticed
How much the snow piles up all winter, did you?"

"Well, no. I worked all day. You can't sit down
And waste good time at work to watch the snow."

"You trying to say there's no work here?"

                                        "Oh, now."

"You found out what it's like stuck here with nothing
But wind and snow. It's always been like this.
With Christmas on us, it's worse. Rob can't get
Away from work, just like you never could,
And Will is—"

                    "I know, I know. You feel alone.
I understand."

                    "No, I don't feel alone.
For years, all sorts of company's come to call:
Possums up in the walls, raccoons in vents,
Snakes in the basement, these mice in the cabinets,
That cat that had her kittens in the garage."

"You didn't mind the cats."

                              "They didn't stay."

"Stayed long enough for me. Damn things were feral.
Every time you picked one up, it bit you."

"They didn't bite me. They bit you."

                                   "All right.
I'll have to be your company now. OK?"

"Have to?" She lined some cans up on the counter

Angled between them. "You make it sound like work."

"How come you're reading into what I say?"

"I'm not. It's work for you to stay inside.
Just look. You sit there, staring out the window."

"I like to watch the birds come to the feeder.
I like the way they fly off in the woods.
Rob misses snow, and birds. I ought to call him."

"He'll be at work. It's two in California."

"I know. Just think he'd like to hear about it.
If I'd have cleared the brush back from the woods,
Then I could see more birds."

        "Why do you want
To cut things back so much? You mowed all summer,
Stacked brush, pruned trees. You went and baled that hay,
And we don't keep livestock."

        "I sold that hay.
Besides, you weed things out, then what all's left
Can grow back strong."

        "How can you say such things?"

"I don't know. I don't know what it is I've said."

"How can you not know? You retired then worked
Outside all day while I took care of Will."

"I said I'd hire you help."

        "That's not my point.
Will sat and watched the trees, he watched the fields,
He watched you with those men from up the road,

Cutting the hay before you went and hauled it
In bales like little boxes. I watched you too."

"But don't you like how smooth the fields look now?
You keep things neat, they're easy to take care of.
If you'd keep up your cabinets, when the mice
Got in them, they wouldn't be a chore."

                                        "Oh, please.
You keep your tools on hooks. You keep things labeled.
That doesn't mean I should."

                            "But when you square
Away your things, you can forget about them."

"I know. That's how you were when Will was here.
You hardly talked to him, like he was gone
Before he was gone. I've watched you keep things
Cut, clean, and neat, then you forget about them."

"I'd like just once to speak my mind without
You twisting what I say into some symbol."

"Where are you going?"

                        "I'm putting on my boots.
Do you know why I wanted to call Rob?
I bet you don't. I'd like to tell somebody
What I saw in the field without somebody
Making more of it, like you'll do if I tell you."

"So, tell me."

                        "Cat prints. They trailed along the fence,
Down to the road, over to the mailbox,
Then up across the field. They stopped right there,

Like they'd been drifted over. But they weren't.
There was, more than a yard across, these wingprints,
An owl's, I guess, pressed down into the snow.
Make of that what you will."

                              "By telling me
You couldn't tell me, you've made something of it."

He stared out at the dark then laced his boots.
"Mail should've come by now."

                                        He snatched his coat,
Stepped past her, and since she couldn't keep him there,
She called out after him: "When you get back,
I'll need you to come set the traps for me."

SALT OF THE EARTH

The metro editor I called Fish threw
His weight into the roadhouse door until
It gave and, with the blowing snow, he sprawled
Inside. "Goddammit, shut the goddamn door,"
A voice called, and I did.

                    "Aw, leave it. Hell,"
Another voice said, "warmer out than in."

Fish waved a greeting, but the barman peered,
Toweled off his hands, then leaned in toward his patrons.
Still wrapped in coats and hats, the people stared
And wouldn't speak, until we'd scuttled back
To where pool tables hunkered under lights.
We sat, cold beers arrived, and Fish said, "Man,
I love this place. Real people here, you know?"
Off to my left, two men—one old, gray-haired,
The other young and strong, but drunk—shot nine ball,
Each vying for the kitty on their table.
"Salt of the earth," Fish said. "You hang out here,
You get to see what's real. You get the truth."

The paper had been put to bed, and I'd
Told Fish I had a six-hour drive to get
Back home for Christmas. He'd insisted, though,
And if I didn't join him, he'd remember.

"What do you mean?" I said.

                    "The truth. Real people.
Real truth. Like what we write, right?"

Something bumped
My foot, and I looked down, then up, to see
The drunk point with his cue. "Nice boots," he said.
"I got boots just like that, but mine got Gore-Tex.
You going hunting, man, you need the Gore-Tex."

"Hey, pretty boy," the old man called. "Your shot."

"I'm history," the drunk said, then he staggered
Back to the game.

                    "Salt of the earth," Fish said.
He grinned. I drank and looked off toward the bar,
Where one taped, yellowed photocopy said,
It's hard to soar with eagles when you work . . .
The final phrase was blocked by rows of bottles.

The drunk returned. He stared. He finally spoke:
"Whatchyou guys do?"

                    "We write," Fish said.

                                        "No shit.
Huh. Whatchyou write?"

                    "Write for the *Times*."

                                        "No shit.
Man, I'm a welder. Know what I do?"

                                "What?"

"I weld."

          "Hey, pretty boy," the old man called.

"They fired my ass today. Hey, you guys write.
I got this story for you. Here's your headline:

Welder Gets Canned." The drunk swayed, stepped, then leaned
Against his cue.

                "Sorry there, bud," Fish said.
"That's not a story. Happens all the time."

"I ain't done yet," the drunk said. Then he tucked
The cuestick to his shoulder, gripped it, aimed.
"Welder Gets Canned," he said again, then jabbed
His stick at Fish's breastbone. "Locks and Loads."

"Hey, pretty boy," the old man yelled, and then
He stuck the winnings in his coat. "You lose."
The drunk whirled, swung his stick. The old man ducked,
Shoving the young man at the corner cue rack,
Which splintered like a sheaf of wheat. "Get up,"
The old man said, and so the drunk tried, fell,
Then scrabbled out the back. Snow sifted in
And spread across the tiles.

                   "Would someone shut
The goddamn door?" the voice called. Fish just stared
At his white Oxford shirt, a round blue stain
Over his heart.

          "Ready?" I said. He nodded.
We paid, leaving the way the drunk had gone.
I checked to see the door stayed shut behind us.

II

STRIPPER

Along the tourist strip up from the dam,
We two boys wandered, ogling storefront windows
Where leather goods and T-shirts hung like ducks,
And busts of Christ were chainsawed out of oak.
We passed the cage where freaks ate snakes, cages
Where men struck fastballs while their women waited.
We went to the arcade, played pinball, Skee-Ball,
And eyed, back in the corner, a machine
The sign said we weren't old enough to touch.
And so my brother shoved a quarter in.
Above the rifle, this word—*Stripper*—pulsed.
Inside, a scratched slide of a woman glared.
One hand on her cocked hip, she smiled at us
Like she knew us but was oblivious of
The black dot on her arm at which my brother
Fired. When he missed, he fired again and struck.
A different woman, stripped of her blouse, gleamed.
A raucous volley followed. Each slide revealed
More and more women posed behind the glass,
Their hands on knees or breasts or reaching out,
Their faces grim or grinning as my brother
Took aim at every target, picking off
Hair ribbons, bra, skirt, shoes and stockings, garters,
Until one woman stood, stripped to her panties,
The target steady, her breasts thrust toward us in
A confrontation boys knew little of,
Her lips forming an O I thought voiced pain.
The last shot laid her down. The screen went black.

We hurried out the back door toward the darkness.
But then there were the cries of whippoorwills,
The docklights trembling on the distant lake,
A concrete walkway leading to a maze
Hacked out of hedges, a sprawling topiary
Where playful screams and cloying laughter rose
From couples who'd discovered they were lost.

UNDERTOW

Hard rains had cut the river road in half,
So Tanner, me, and Brain, whose name was Brian
But we called Brain because he was dyslexic,
Slogged from the truck then down along the bank
To do what we'd each bet the other wouldn't.
We stripped. We shivered from the chill. "Ain't cold,"
Brain said.

       "You're drunk," I said.

                    "No more than you."

"So like I said," I said. We stood awhile,
Waiting as if we listened for a voice
To call us to the water. Only leaves
Of cottonwoods hissed overhead, though some
Dropped in the current where they were swept away,
Or under. "I can't see why she'd divorce you,"
I said to Tanner, who stared out at the bluffs
Waiting across the river.

              "Horseshit," Brain said.
"When she was carrying on at the reception,
Doing that money dance with everybody,
We bet ten bucks it wouldn't last a year."

"River's up," said Tanner. He took one step
Into the water. "Last fall we'd have these fights.
I'd drive down here to get some air. One time
I saw two cattle caught out in an eddy.

They bawled until the water plucked them down.
That river's nice to look at, like a woman,
But don't trust what you see."

                              "Never," Brain said,
"Trust anything that bleeds a week and lives."

"That's sick. No wonder you can't get a date."

"Brainy, you got it backwards," Tanner said.

"What other way you think he's gonna get it?"

"No. Listen," Tanner said. "I was a kid,
I'd swim the jetty pools, and so I thought
When I got older I was strong enough
To swim the river. God. It dragged me down
So far so fast I didn't know what happened,
But I could hear rocks click like teeth; it scraped me
Across its bed, spun me around, and then,
Like that, it let me go. I coughed up mud
For days, and even now, I'll have these dreams
Some nights and wake up kicking at my covers
Just as it drags me down." He thumped his chest
And waded in waist deep before he turned.
"So you boys up for this?"

                              "What boys?" Brain said.
"Just who you think you're calling boys?"

                                        Tanner
Threw back his head and filled the trees with laughter.
We stood up straight and waded for the water.

PARADISE, MISSOURI

I paced. I looked at thumbtacked prints of Christ
Down in the nursery of the Baptist Church:
Christ raising Lazarus, scolding disciples,
Or suffering children to come unto him.
My groomsmen sat, drank beer, and talked too much.

"When you got fitted for that tux," Josh said,
"Did you get fitted for a ball and chain?"

"Hey man, once you get married," David said,
"You won't believe how many chicks'll want you."

"We should have gone back out to Paradise,"
Ralph Yale said. "Like we did before my wedding."

"Don't tell this now," I said.

                          "Why not?" he said.
"We drove out to that shotgun shack Mike Hall had—
Liquor in troughs and bags of dope like snacks,
And God, there were these girls up from the lake.
Man of the hour here gets messed up so bad
He mashes with this one. Turns out she's married.
Hell, you'd been dating Julia, what? A year?"

"You're one to talk," I said. "You got married
Just one week later. What'd you do that night?"

"Yeah, yeah. So they're right by her husband's truck.
Course, hubby kicks the hell out of our boy,
Until Mike pulls him off, right?"

                              "I don't know."

Late amber light blazed through one window well,
The stink of perfume and soured milk grew strong,
And while they kept on about Paradise,
Its recent dam, its shotgun shacks, its store
Where we, as boys, bought stinkbait and tobacco,
Then went down to the river, I ignored them,
But when I tried to crack a window, saw
This print of Jesus in Gethsemane,
Down on his knees before the soldiers came
And Judas kissed his cheek and Peter lopped
The ear of Malchus off. And I recalled
She wasn't pretty. "He gets drunk," she'd said.
"He even hit me just for eating french fries
In his new truck. I bet you're not like that."
We'd leaned against an old outhouse in back,
Her lips against my neck, my hands inside
Her shirt, until she had me follow her.
Again, her lips, and then a shot of light
Ripped through my skull, and I dropped to the road
Taking kick after kick. All I could see
Was the lit billboard glaring near the store:
Last stop before the lake—liquor, bait,
And ammo.

                    "What was that girl's name?" Ralph said.

"I don't know," I said.

                         Then someone upstairs
Called, and my groomsmen stood, and we filed out
Into the sanctuary of cut flowers
And organ swells and fading, glass-stained light.

In the Neighborhood

Startled awake on New Year's Day, I bitched
About the hoots and hollers, screams, the *pop-*
Pop-popping, which, at first, I took for fireworks.
"I mean, what's there to celebrate?" I said
Then turned my back to her and tried to sleep.
She laughed, and now that time has passed between us,
I think that laugh was laced with some sad malice.
Come spring, we spaded up the beds and found
A hollow-point slug from a .38
Sunk in the loam. She left it on the stoop.
The days grew warm, and we pushed up the windows,
So when a meth house cropped up one block west,
Each night we'd hear the cries of wacked-out tweakers,
The crack of fistfights, blaring horns of addicts
Craving their fix, and traffic speeding past
Our corner, heedless of the signs and limits.
The cops were useless. That house didn't sell
Enough to trouble them, they said, so we'd
Sit on the porch, keeping our lists of cars
And license plates, though often she'd start fretting
For these two girls, who, well into each evening,
Would rollerblade straight through our intersection.
One time, she called out after them to please,
Just look both ways. They laughed and skated on.
I was amused, though, by our jobless neighbor
Who owned no car, and thus each evening pedaled
His six-year-old son's bike down to our corner,
Searching for signs the dealer was at home.

Back and then forth he'd go, his legs so long
His knees would bump against the handlebars.
One morning on my way to work I saw
The bike abandoned in the meth-house yard.
Later, and inexplicably, hundreds
Of brand-new sharpened kitchen knives were found
Strewn down the block and onto lawns, so cops
Put crime tape up to keep the kids away.
Fall came. One night we lay in bed, not touching,
Just listening to the wind and our own breathing,
Until, from one block west, a woman shouted,
"You don't know love."

                       "Do so," a man yelled back.

"You don't," the woman argued. "You don't know love.
You don't even know how to spell love."

                             "Do too,"
The man cried out. "Love. L-O-V-E. Love."

This time, she turned. This time, she tried to sleep.
This time, I was the one compelled to laugh
At just one more thing in the neighborhood.

ORNAMENTS

Thanksgiving day was over, and she'd gone,
On business, out of town. The scent of sage,
Yeast bread, and nutmeg lingered; tapered candles
Set on the mantel stood, wicks black and shriveled;
And that house swelled so violently with warmth
Joists popped, cracking the silence that remained.
I read the paper in the dining room,
But when snow started falling, I decided
I'd hang some ornaments for her return.
Down in the basement, one bare bulb revealed
The stacks of decorations, which I cradled
So high I didn't see an errant box
Laid in my path until I kicked it over—
Postcards and envelopes. Her work address.
A stranger's tidy script. A local postmark
Dated these past two years. Some things, we know
Before we know. But still, I read those letters:
The adolescent prattle of a man
Whose thoughts on love were muddled by clichés.
Her eyes, he wrote, were *deep as wells;* her lips
Tasted like honey. He reveled in what he,
Three times, referred to as *womanly wiles.*
I put the letters back then hauled each box
Of ornaments up to the living room.
Snow ticked against the panes. I caught my breath.
I walked out through the cold, started the car,
And ended up at the museum of art,

Where people would be so engrossed in lives
Diminished, straightened up, enlightened, framed,
They wouldn't notice my slack-jawed self-pity.
I wandered hallways, listening to kids' sneakers
Squeaking on marble floors and one squat guard
Crinkling a coughdrop wrapper and three old women
Rambling about light's value, until I saw
Saint Lawrence, who, on orders from the Pope,
Passed out the Church's treasures to the poor
But angered Emperor Valerian,
Who claimed the wealth and ordered Lawrence roasted.
I stared, and even when the squat guard coughed,
Clearing his throat, announcing the museum
Would close in just ten minutes, I kept staring:
Back in the oily darkness, two men whispered;
Behind the flames, a fat man pumped the bellows;
Out from a wall of smoke, a wart-faced fool
Loomed, grinned, and carted kindling for the grill
While in the spotlit foreground, Lawrence knelt.
He seemed a boy, thin whiskers on his cheek,
His raiment stripped; a guard bent back his arm
And kneed his spine so Lawrence had to stare
Toward heaven, where there was only rising smoke
In which, soon, he would rise. That's love, I thought,
That mindless acquiescence. Let lovers have it.
Then guards began to line up, blocking the hall.
They strolled along with fabricated patience,
Sweeping us stragglers toward the doors and out
To where snow angled through the streetlamps' glow.
I leaned into each gust. I winced and squinted.
Still, I could see how everything was covered.

H A B I T

These days, my friends keep taking me to lunch.
Last Friday, Leigh and Richard—wife and husband—
Met me at this place on the boulevard.
We sat outside and ordered wine and tapas.
I faced the angling sun and railroad tracks
That run behind Royal Liquors, where, sometimes,
Illegal aliens hop down from cars
And disappear. When silence tailed a question
Richard had posed to me, I glimpsed a man
Who stumbled from behind the liquor store
But lost him in the traffic's glare. Then Leigh
Spoke through my silence:

                              "You read the *Star* today?
How some guy wants to buy that Bob, oh, what,
What's his last name?"

                              "Berdella," Richard said.
"Berdella *was* his last name."

                              "Yes, Berdella.
Some rich guy wants to buy Berdella's house
And all the stuff he tortured those boys with."

Richard had simply asked me what friends ask:
"How could you not have seen it happening?"

"I don't know what was there to see," I say.
What I won't tell most couples is, amidst
The rituals of work and sleep and waking,

I thought love was a given, although love
Is like the habits of our days. Or our days.

"We lived two houses down from him," Leigh said.

"Three houses," Richard said.

                              "Whatever. Three.
We'd both just graduated. I know that.
And married. And neither of us had a job."

I looked away from them. A waiter snapped
A tablecloth; a straggling businessman
Studied his check, then tipped and stood to go,
And then I caught that stranger wavering
Across the street, one hand outstretched to ward
The passing cars away, the other hand
Pressed to his temple as if he were thinking.

"Rich and I'd lay out on the deck," Leigh said.
"But some days when the wind was blowing right,
There'd be this smell. Rich thought it was a dog,
One that got hit and crawled somewhere to die."

"Leigh bugged me to go find it," Richard said.

"He wouldn't, though."

                              "Well, what could I have done?"

"Nothing," Leigh said. "The odor went away.
Until that boy jumped from Berdella's attic—
Remember? Someone saw him on the street,
Drugged out, a collar on? His leg was broke?—
Until they saved that boy and searched the house
And found those Polaroids and ropes and dug
That backyard up, we never even knew."

Leigh drained her wine. Then Richard cleared his throat.
Behind me, silverware crashed in a tub.
The sun was so low all that I could see
Was that man coming—dark skin, matted hair,
Hand to his head that looked as if he'd crushed
Red roses there. He stumbled at the curb.
"Excuse me," he said. "Please. Excuse me. Please."
He leaned with his free hand, rocking our table,
Then held his hand up, out, to make us stay.
"I'm sorry," he finally said then turned and wove
Across the boulevard. A drop of blood
Had spattered on our table. I stared at it.

"Well, that was something," Leigh said.

Maybe it was,
I tried to say. Maybe, I hoped, it wasn't.

TRANSFER

Three-quarters through a one-year lease I watched
A carnival rise from the strip-mall lot
Across the four-lane, then, as if I worked
In concert with those harried carnies, I hauled
Some still-packed boxes down to basement storage.
The transfer that had put me in that complex
Had been a lateral move, yet I'd accepted,
Telling her I'd be foolish not to take it.
"I understand," she said, which meant, "It's over,"
Words I'd not said because I lacked the mercy
To put us each out of our misery,
Though that was what we shared, and that was what,
The longer I lived in that one-bed, one-bath,
Became my own: the fat, phlegmatic woman
Cooing to her two schnauzers while she swept
Leaves from the walk; the pool where tenants preened;
The smoke from dope and burnt grilled cheese drifting
Up through the floor; and muffled noise: flushed toilets,
Squabbles crescendoing into a crash
Of stainless pans, and my new neighbor's music
Thumping so late at night I lay in bed
Mistaking the low pulsing for my heart.
That night, however, I'd arranged a date,
My second with a woman from the office.
Instead of getting ready, though, I leaned
Against my sliding-glass-door entry, noting
How that black lot filled up with garish light
And tinny music from a time long past—

"The Yellow Rose of Texas," "Shenandoah,"
"Amazing Grace," all heaving double-time
Up from the carousel, over and over,
Until my nerves wore thin, and so I left.
My date returned with me past one a.m.
The lot was quiet, but the rides still glowed,
And so we watched them, while she talked and talked.
Then, finally, silence led us to my bedroom,
Where, in awhile, she asked, did I hear that?
"I can't, you know," she said. "With someone's music
Going while we're, you know." I said I did,
Then got half dressed and went to see my neighbor.
He'd slid his door and curtain back, so light
Poured out while I looked in. I glimpsed bare walls,
A stereo, an unrolled sleeping bag,
And one worn pea-green armchair where he sat,
Eyes closed, and faced me. His brown hair was thinning.
He wore a V-neck T-shirt, khakis, black socks.
He held a cigarette in his right hand,
But with his left, he beat time on the chair arm,
Mouthing the lyrics to the Allman Brothers'
"Ramblin' Man." I had to look away,
And when I did, the carnival went dark
As if it wasn't there at all. That night,
I let his music fill our common wall.

Human Resources

Gabe handed me a beer and slapped my shoulder:
"It's good to hear you get back in the game."

"I said she's pretty. I didn't say I want
To play the game."

                    "Well, who do you think does?"

I looked around: low light, blue smoke, dark wood,
The import beer on special; men had stripped
Their jackets, loosened ties; they eyed the women
Still dressed in suits and low-heeled pumps, and most
Were gathered at the long bar mirror, where they
Could glance at someone glancing back at them.

"Which one is she?" Gabe said.

                              I gave a nod.

"God, yes. Good choice. She's got a fat friend, though.
They always got fat friends. How 'bout you take
The fat one? I'll take her."

                         "You're funny, Gabe."

"I'm kidding you. Go introduce yourself."
Dark wavy hair pulled back, pale neck, blue eyes,
A little too much lipstick for my taste,
But still . . . "She just looked at you."

                              "She did not."

"Hell yeah, she did, and then she licked her lips,
Like this. Now, what you do is go say hi,
Trade business cards, then scoot. You're safe that way.
There won't be any weirdos call your home,
And you can screen them out at work. I mean,
What we got here's the dregs: new divorcées
With open wounds, unmarrieds no one wants,
And folks off work who want to just get drunk."

"So where do we fit in?"

                              "Go talk to her."

I did. The fat friend walked away from us.
We chatted for awhile, and then she dug
Into her purse and handed me her card.
She was a human resource manager.
She said she did some of the company's hiring.
"You like that?" I said.

                         "I'm a people person,"
She said. "So, like, I do. My first job, though?
I hated it. For this phone company?
I had to leave."

               I asked her why that was.
She stared like I was some job candidate
Then cocked her head and smiled. My gut got tight.

"You're probably not the kind who'll want to hear this,
But it was all those damn minorities.
They don't like work, and we still had to hire them."
She paused. "Like, do you have a card?" she said.
"I have to find my friend."

"I'm out," I said.

She shrugged, wished me goodnight, then left me there.
Gabe stood with one young woman at the bar,
And they were laughing. Two men brushed against me.
"Before you get too drunk," one said, "those girls
Are really fat."

"That one's got big tits, though,"
The other said.

"Yeah, that's because she's fat."

I read her card again. I drained my beer.
The men moved on, and I could see my face
Between some other faces in the mirror.

C OMMUTE

Each weeknight as I walked to my apartment,
My grease-stained work clothes reeking of dried sweat,
My steeltoes clopping on the walk, my keys
Clicking against my thigh, wool-suited men
And well-groomed women looked away from me,
Knowing my place, which, mornings, was the train.
I'd board past five a.m. with other men,
Grunt laborers like me. I hated them:
Young men in fraying jackets, backward caps,
Walkmans that hissed like snakes; and men my age
With grease-gray hands and *USA Today*s
And brown, tumescent lunch sacks set beside them;
And ancient, snoring men, their heads thrown back
As if they'd waited for the razor's edge.
I'd turn away from them, only to find
Their pale reflections wavering on the glass.
Or sometimes I would doze until the train
Lurched from the station. Webs of gray rail vanished
In fog swept off the bay, then crossing-gates
Clanged crazily, their red lights flashed, warning
Nothing but darkness into which the train
Clicked faster, heading out toward Tunnel One.
On winter mornings, scattered fires were built there.
Men lurked there too, curled up on bedrolls, papers,
And cardboard mats, though once, beside the tracks,
Three men stood by their fire; another crouched.
A dog wove in between them while I watched
The squatting man tip a bottle to his lips.

Across the aisle, these two old men who shared
A copy of the *Chronicle* each morning,
Jabbered above the clatter of the train.
One shook his pages, said, "What are you, Ilus?"

"What's that?"

                "What are you? I said. What's your sign?"

"Hell, I don't know."

                "Well, what's your birthdate then?"

"March thirteenth. Why you wanna know?"

                      "Because."

Out on the stony flat, that man's tall bottle
Glowed in the amber firelight as he drank.
Or seemed to drink. He set the bottle down
Then spat into the coals so one sharp flame
Burst forth as if it issued from the earth.
The dog shied back, the squatter grinned, looked up,
And one of those three yelled, I swear, at me.
The squatter raised his fist and flipped me off.
What could I do? I did the same to him
Before the train passed into Tunnel One.
Darkness. My face. My fist. My upright finger
Reflected on the pane until I turned
And the commuter screeched to its first stop.
The dark was fading. Walls of fog fell back,
But on the train, the two old men kept talking:
"Why you wanna know, I said."

"And I said,
Because. It says right here feelings of oneness
Will overtake you."

"What's that?"

"I said it says
Feelings of oneness, today, will overtake you."

"Hm," Ilus said. "Ain't nothin' new 'bout that."

TRUE STORY

"True story," Rome Romano shouted down
From where he'd climbed and belted thirty feet
Up on a pole beside the main line, running
Through garlic fields near Gilroy, California.
"True story," he called out to our gang that stood
Below because most of us hated climbing:
Gaffs rattling on your legs like braces, points
Sinking in wood, your ass and tool belt swaying.
But Rome liked it. He liked to get away
From us and see the things we couldn't see:
Laborers hunching through the distant rows,
The carcass of a dog, abandoned spurs,
A family boiling clothes beside a boxcar,
All that, while Smith and Sandoval recalled
This girl they'd spoken to at 7-Eleven:

"Good God, she had big tits."

                         "Shit yeah, she did.
I can't believe you asked if she knew where
There was a Pic 'n' Save. You're one sad fuck."

"Just making conversation."

                         "She doesn't shop
At Pic 'n' Save."

                 "She bought a cup of coffee
At 7-Eleven."

                 "It's a convenience store."

"Well, I'd convenience her."

"You would."

"I would."

"I said you would."

"True story," Rome said again.
He cleared his throat, held one hand to the sky.
"The day after the shuttle crashed," he said,
"I was in Fresno County working fields
In fog that was like hands clapped to your eyes.
But when the fog burned off, somebody saw
Something bumping against a canal grate.
A log, we thought. 'Looks like a birch,' I said,
Pale as it was. But there weren't birches there.
Then someone said it's just a cotton bale,
Then PVC pipe, someone said, a tarp,
A cable spool. No one would go and check.
A mannequin, I said. Well, we got quiet.
This sheriff came and leaned against his car
Then crossed his arms like this. Three guys in masks
And rubber gloves and hip boots waded out.
They dragged a woman to the bank. She wore
A gold watch, heels, but you could see her throat
Was cut. God, no one said a word until
This sheriff yelled, 'Is it an astronaut?'"

Rome got his line wrench, tightened up the crossbolt.
We stared at Rome. He wouldn't look our way.
But when Smith started laughing Rome hurled down
His wrench and nicked him on the shoulder. "True story,"
Rome said. "That's a true story."

                         "When you get down,"
Smith yelled, "you're fucked."

                         Rome leaned back on his belt
And laughed, then spread his arms out to the sky,
So from the ground it looked like he was falling.
"Don't you think I know that? I know that."

TUNNEL ONE

Hawk drove the gang truck down the bayside tracks
While Hondo said that men who lived in camps
Near Tunnel One had stolen copper cable.
Cut it. Carted it off the charred stone walls
To sell for scrap, which left the signal lights
And crossing-gates along the main line dead.
"If we're not done by dark," he said, "they'll sneak
Back here like spooks." Hawk parked far from the hole.
We had to lug our tools and cable past
Blankets and cardboard tents that lay beside
Still-smoking fires. It seemed as if those men
Had sunk into the earth, leaving behind
Old condoms dry as snake skins, shoes, syringes,
And pages torn from porno magazines
That scraped around our feet as a commuter
Blasted into the hole. We followed, playing
Lights down the wall until we found the breach
Where these words had been sprayed: *I am distracted.*
Thy fierce wrath goeth over me, thy terrors
Have cut me off. Psalms 88:16.
Below the verse someone had scratched, *fuck that.*
We measured out new cable, stripped it, spliced
Until lunchtime when Hondo led us out
Above the hole, beneath an overpass,
Back to a piece of plywood he pushed over,
Revealing a dugout room, a mattress, candles,
And on one wall a spray-paint mural of
A grinning, naked girl. Her legs were spread.

Snakes coiled around her ankles. Spiders crawled
Across her thighs, and just below one breast
Her painted flesh looked like a scroll rolled back.
Out from behind her cage of bones a hand
Gave us the finger.

                All afternoon, we worked,
Then Hondo sent Hawk out to check the signals.
Twilight had hauled in fog like concrete slabs
At each end of the tunnel, so Hawk was just
A silhouette when he came running back,
Yelling about a man between the rails.
"I kicked his foot to see if he was dead,"
Hawk said. "He laughed at me. What should we do?"

"He'll get up if he wants to," Hondo said.
"Go back down there and watch the signals."

                            "We can't
Just leave him there."

                "Like hell we can't."

                         Hawk shrugged
And walked away until a train's headlight
Swelled in the fog, and then he ran and waved
His arms to the commuter while it bore
Into the tunnel, scattering dust, pressing
Us back to search the rails and grating wheels
For blood or cloth, some remnant of that man.
But even as the last car left the tunnel,
Hawk kept on running. Then a figure stood,
A man who shook his fist our way and danced
A jig into the fog until he vanished.

SOLIDARITY

The ditch we'd dug all morning in hard rain
Had caved in, catching Smith up to his gut
In mud and stones. We tried to pull him out,
But all the while, he bitched until I joked
That we should leave him. So we did. We hunkered
Under a tarp draped over two black stacks
Of creosote-soaked ties and watched him struggle,
But when he yelled how he was sinking deeper,
We went back, picked and shoveled, mocked his sniveling,
Then trudged back to our shelter. No one said much,
Except for Smith, who ranted until Hondo
Told him to shut up.

                    "What do you mean shut up?"

"What do you mean what do I mean? Shut up."

"Make me."

                    "Make you? Yeah, right. I'm the lead man."

While those two rattled on, I said to Baze,
Our newest grunt, who lived up in the city,
That last night I'd gone down to Castro Street
And watched the Halloween festivities:
Men sporting plastic phalluses or breasts;
Men dressed in chaps; men draped in long black habits—
The Sisters of Perpetual Indulgence—
Wending a maypole dance between the gawkers.

Smith turned. "You a faggot?"

                         I said I'd seen
Up on a fire escape equipped with mikes
This black queen in a sea-foam, sequined number
Belting out "Respect," while down the stairway
Men chorused, "Sock it to me, sock it to me . . ."

"Well, are you?"

                    "I saw that," Baze said. "I was there."

"Two faggots," Smith said.

                      "I'm married," Baze said. "Kids."

"That makes a difference?"

                    "No way," Hondo said.
"Faggots think one hole's same as any other."

"How do you know?" I said.

                "Hey, yeah," Smith said,
"How do you?" We laughed.

                  "Shut up. We all know that."

"He is right," Smith said. "All those queer parades?
That's twisted."

              "Twisted," Baze said, then he nodded.
"When I was back in high school, there's this kid—
Vance Evans—great ballplayer, killer cannon.
He's in the shower. Whole team's in the shower.
Well, Evans pops a boner. Tries to hide it.
When he gets out, we crack him with our towels

So hard we cut him. He slips. We leave him there.
We called him Boner so much after that
He quit, and—"

       "Hell, in this bar once," Hondo said,
"Faggot comes up behind me, grabs my ass.
I whipped around and tagged him. Laid him out."

The clouds seemed lower then; wind shook the tarp,
Letting the hard rain pummel our huddled gang.
"Well, he deserved it then," Baze said. "Some guy
Chooses your sorry ass deserves what he gets."

"Ah hah," Smith said. "He got you there."

               "Shut up.
Ain't nothing wrong with my ass."

               "How come you're worried
What we think of your ass?" I said.

               "And you,
You shut the fuck up too. I'm the lead man."

S E N I O R I T Y

"Hey, little girls," our lead man Hondo yelled
From where he stood above the ditch we'd dug
In steady drizzle down across the main line.
I looked up, heaved a shovelful of mud
Close to his feet as I could get, then glimpsed
Four schoolgirls dressed in matching uniforms
Cutting across the tracks. Just west, lights strung
In bay trees near the drag of stores and coiled
Around foil stars screwed into lampposts glowered.
"Hey, little girls," he yelled again then wagged
The handle of a pick between his legs.
"You want some candy little girls?"

                                    "Shut up,"
I said and tossed more muck. He threw his pick
Aside and stared.

                        "You got some kinda problem?"
"Yeah, leave the girls alone."

                                    "It's just a joke,"
Hawk said. "Relax."

                        I looked east of the tracks
To where a floodlit reach of asphalt packed
With sports cars gleamed, and there, an edifice
Of vaulted windows glowed, and I could see,
Because the skies were foul and business slow,
Salesmen kept pacing, watching us at work.

"Yeah, just relax. And while you're at it, dig.
Sooner you get us off the main line, sooner
I get the backhoe, sooner we get gone."

Cars hissed past; laden shoppers hustled home,
But jobs were scarce, and in that giving season
Money was scarcer, and so on we dug,
Until, trying to change the mood, Hawk said,
"Let's say you could have just one thing for Christmas,
Forget about the cost, what would you want?
Myself, I'd get me one of those Mercedes.
Then I could go where I want, when I want."

"I'd get my wife a boob job," Hondo said.

"Charming," I said.

                 "Screw you. What would you want?"

"Dry socks. A different job. With my luck, though,
Some other guy like you would be in charge."

We laughed, but Hondo walked off in a huff,
Climbed up the backhoe, revved it, spun its wheels
So hard it sank, then jerked it through the lot,
Flipping thick crud across the pristine asphalt.
We laid pipe, backfilled, and he scraped his ditch
Until a salesman strode from that cathedral
And waited where the asphalt met our mud.
Hondo climbed down, walked over to the man,
Who spoke, gesticulated, then stormed off.
"Go sweep that shit up," Hondo said to me.
While drizzle changed to rain and salesmen stood
Beneath their awning, crossed their arms, and, laughing,

Pointed out spots I'd missed, I cleaned their lot.
Back in the truck, the gang sat snug and warm.
Hondo called out the window: "Merry Christmas."

"The socks," I yelled back. "What about the socks?"

He held one arm out to the rain and shrugged:
"Only so much a guy like me can do."

THE SIGNALMEN

Our gang dug down two feet. With two feet left,
Our shovels scratched at oblong cobblestones,
The remnant of some street to Sunnyvale.
We strained our backs, heaving out stones by hand,
Then where we could, we dug deep, laying pipe
In which we'd run the wire to each new signal.
That was the day that Paul Gonzales drove
Too fast along the main line to our ditch
And told us that he'd seen a girl struck dead
By a commuter on the eastbound main
Near milepost thirty-six. He'd been called out
To check a switch and saw some schoolgirls cut
Across the tracks. But one girl wouldn't cross
Until the others teased her. The bike she pushed
Caught on the rails. "Worked more than forty years,"
Gonzales said. "Got two months left to go.
I tell you. I don't need to see that shit."
Our foreman kicked a clod off of a stone
And said, "When I worked down in San Jose,
There was this woman hid between the rails.
Nobody saw her. Then a freight came on,
And she sat up as straight as Lazarus.
Wasn't a goddamn thing we could have done."
He shook his head then looked up from the stone.
"Hot rail," he said. We climbed out of the ditch
And watched the train approach. From far away,
We saw the black cowcatcher where the cops
Had marked the girl's form—trunk, arms, legs—with tape.

We smelled the diesel smoke. We felt the heat.
Wheels squalled, cars clamored, the commuters stared
Down through the dusty windows. We stared back.
The dirt we'd dug kicked up and danced around us
Then settled when the final car wailed past.

HUMAN

"You make mistakes," Smith said. "I make mistakes.
All of us make mistakes, but listen." We couldn't.
As Smith bitched, waggling a three-pound hammer
He'd hustled back across the line to fetch,
An Amtrak wailed by. Still, his jaw worked on
Until the last car clacked past. Then he kicked
The faulty bond he'd welded to the web
And had to chisel free to weld again
Before he asked, "Know what I mean?" We did.
He'd worn us down with his tired diatribe:
How Hawk, because he'd failed a random piss test,
Shouldn't be granted a three-month suspension
With benefits and pay, but should, instead,
Be fired. "The rules are rules," he said. "No drugs."

"Christ's sake," Baze said. "Guy's got a wife and kids.
You want to make it worse for them?"

                                        "For them?
He drives the gang truck. What if he's all stoned
And hits a tree and one of us gets killed?"

"Depends on who gets killed," Baze said.

                                "What's that mean?"

With one less man our work had gone too slow,
And we were dead, or almost, on our hours,
Working some tangled switchyard in the midst
Of a decrepit landscape strange to us:

A place where what we thought were three whores hailed us
From a graffitied overpass; where transients,
As freights bore down, wove drunk across the tracks,
Making their way to lean-tos and low fires;
And where, all day, through-trains we weren't expecting
Caught us close to the tracks and off our guard.

"Nothing," Baze said. "Means I wouldn't mind doing
Some drugs myself."

                    "But see, you don't. Hawk did.
And by all rights, they oughta fire his ass."

"He's only human."

                    "So? I'm human too."

Baze shook his head; Smith cursed the chisel he'd left
Back in his bag, then stormed across the tracks.
Some saw the coming freight; some yelled hot rail.
Smith, though, was pissed and yapping to himself,
So Baze ran down the bed, snatched Smith's coat collar,
Yanked back, and threw him, scrabbling, to the ballast.

"You asshole," Smith said. "What the hell you think—"

His question, though, was stifled by the engines,
Horn blasts, and wheels against the jointed track.
But when the train was gone, the racket dead,
Smith stood, brushed off his pants, and wavered onward.

"Sorry about that," Baze said. "My mistake."

GOD SHED HIS GRACE

I struggled to read Homer in translation
And keep my hands from trembling with the jolt
Of the commuter back to San Francisco.
I reeked of diesel smoke and creosote.
Sweat rings had stained the ankles of my boots.
Eleven hours and I would rise again
At four a.m., just barely able to make
A fist or hold a cup or grip a shovel.
The reading was a ruse. I craved no knowledge.
I wanted coffee, sleep, tobacco, supper,
And I'd grown tired of reading how that culture
Reveled in glories past and failures coming.
I dozed and woke, dozed. *The Iliad* fell.
I woke, head slick against the rattling pane,
And saw we'd passed Bay Meadows racetrack where
Retirees tottered on; they stunk of beer
And griped about their kids they never saw.
We'd passed Hillsdale; the pretty girls who worked
The shopping mall, offering up perfumes,
Sat still and straight in seats along the aisle.
We'd passed Bayshore; the Vietnamese man
Who each day wavered through the car, his workshirt
Gleaming with sweat and grease, his forearms bright
With metal filings from some tool and die,
Sat with his tiny daughter near the front.
He slept, his head swaying away and back
So that he sometimes brushed against her sleeve.
She didn't care. She stood up in her seat

And sang "America the Beautiful."
Two women back of me said she was *darling*
And *precious* and *an angel*. Storm clouds churned
Across the bay. All day our gang had watched
Them rise but roll no closer to the ditch
We dug by hand. But they came as again
She sang, "O beautiful for spacious skies,
For amber . . . For purple mountain majesties . . .
America, America, God shed. . . ."
Maybe she sang it when her day began
After she'd pledged allegiance in her class.
Or maybe she was proud to learn it through
And sang it once again, not to forget.
One of the women shouted, "Look. Out there.
How the sun's shining on that cloud."

                        "How lovely,"
The other said. "It's like the sky's on fire."
Then hard rain beat the thin walls of the train.
The girl sang louder, battling with the clatter
Of rain and wheels on tracks across the flat
That ran to Tunnel Three. Her father stood
And yelled at her, "Goddammit, you shut up.
I want to sleep. Shut up," and sat back down.
She sobbed and clutched the seat. We hit the tunnel,
Each rider's profile captured in the windows—
Retirees, pretty girls, and worn-out men,
The backs of heads like barley in a breeze.
But faintly, I could hear a woman humming.

CLIMBING

We—Hondo, Sandoval, Smith, Baze, and Hawk—
Pour thermos cups of coffee, chew, and talk
Of weekend projects, football, payday's gains,
And which of that week's labors caused what pains.
Although we mostly dig along the track,
Or else climb poles, Smith says, "I wrenched my back
Doing Hawk's wife, since that boy can't get wood."

"That's true," Hawk says. "She tells me you're real good.
She doesn't feel a thing."

                    Smith spits, Hawk laughs,
And Rome stands up from buckling his gaffs.
He casts a glance their way, but doesn't speak;
Such squalid banter gets us through each week
Of hard rains, diesel smoke, salt-rotten poles
That give way when we climb, and watery holes
We dig ourselves into to earn our keep,
Our food, TV, our warmer place to sleep.
And though it's time to load up and go home,
There's one more wire to cut, and we've picked Rome
To do it, since he's the one who likes to climb.
He gaffs in, breathes deep, then he takes his time.
A train squalls past. Fog crawls the coastal range.
Around us, amber light begins to change.
Rome can't be rushed. This work's his kind of art,
Which might reveal, in time, the human heart,
Or else raise one's thoughts to some greater height.
Or not. Rome digs in like a parasite.

"Well, boys, it's Friday," Smith's compelled to say,
But Rome calls down, "Know what that means? One day
Closer to Monday."

              "That's the fucking shits,"
Smith says. We laugh at him; he turns and spits.
Rome leans back on his belt and folds his arms
Then looks away, out toward the berry farms,
Where laborers hunched all day through sodden rows.
Or maybe he looks at how the main line flows,
Or to the boxcar on a rusted spur
Where a few migrants live. I can't be sure
Just what he sees. He's not the sort who'll tell.
Then he unbelts. His gaffs chime like the bell
Of an old Royal where the margin ends—
Ching-tock, ching-tock, ching—and Rome descends.
Smith yells, "I mean it, Rome, you're one sad fuck."
We gather up our tools. We load the truck.
Rome touches down, into the failing light,
Where all of us stand waiting for the night.

Philip Stephens was educated at the University of Missouri at Columbia, Johns Hopkins University, and the University of California at Irvine. His writing has appeared in such publications as *Agni, Southwest Review, The North American Review,* and *The Oxford American.* He has worked variously as a meter reader, railroad signalman, newspaper reporter, and editor and currently works as a freelance writer in Kansas City, Missouri.